HOW THE APP WORKS

This book includes a free app that allows you to use your smartphone or tablet to see videos and animated scenes on every page. Follow the steps below to download the app and launch it to discover the videos, scenes and sounds from beneath the waves.

1 DOWNLOAD THE APP

The app is available free of charge from the App Store and Google Play. Type in "AtlasOfSeasAndOceans" and look for the icon shown here. Click on it to download the app onto your smartphone or tablet.

2 LAUNCH AND SCAN

Launch the app. You may be asked to authorize access to your camera. Hold your smartphone or tablet over a page. You will see an animated scene with large, bouncy red dots on some illustrations.

3 WATCH, LISTEN, LEARN

Tap the red dots with your finger to trigger the videos. Sit back and enjoy the show! This book has 50 videos and 20 animated scenes.

First published in Great Britain in 2023
by NQ Publishers, an imprint of Nextquisite Ltd
Copyright ©2020 Nextquisite Ltd

All rights reserved. Unauthorized reproduction, in any manner, is prohibited.

Project Director Anne McRae
Illustrations Giulia Quagli
Design Marco Nardi
Text Jamie Collins
Editing Susan Bishop
Consultant Dr. Susanne Harris

Apple and the Apple logo are trademarks of Apple Inc., registered in the U.S. and other countries. App Store is a service mark of Apple Inc.

Google Play and the Google Play logo are trademarks of Google LLC.

*The free **AtlasOfSeasAndOceans** app runs on iOS (11 or later) and Android (7 or later) smartphones and tablets.
iOS: *iPhone* SE, 6s, 6s Plus, 7, 7 Plus, 8, X; all *iPad Pro* models and *iPad* (2017 onwards).
Android: you can find a complete list of compatible devices by scanning this QR code or by visiting https://developers.google.com/ar/discover/supported-devices#google_play

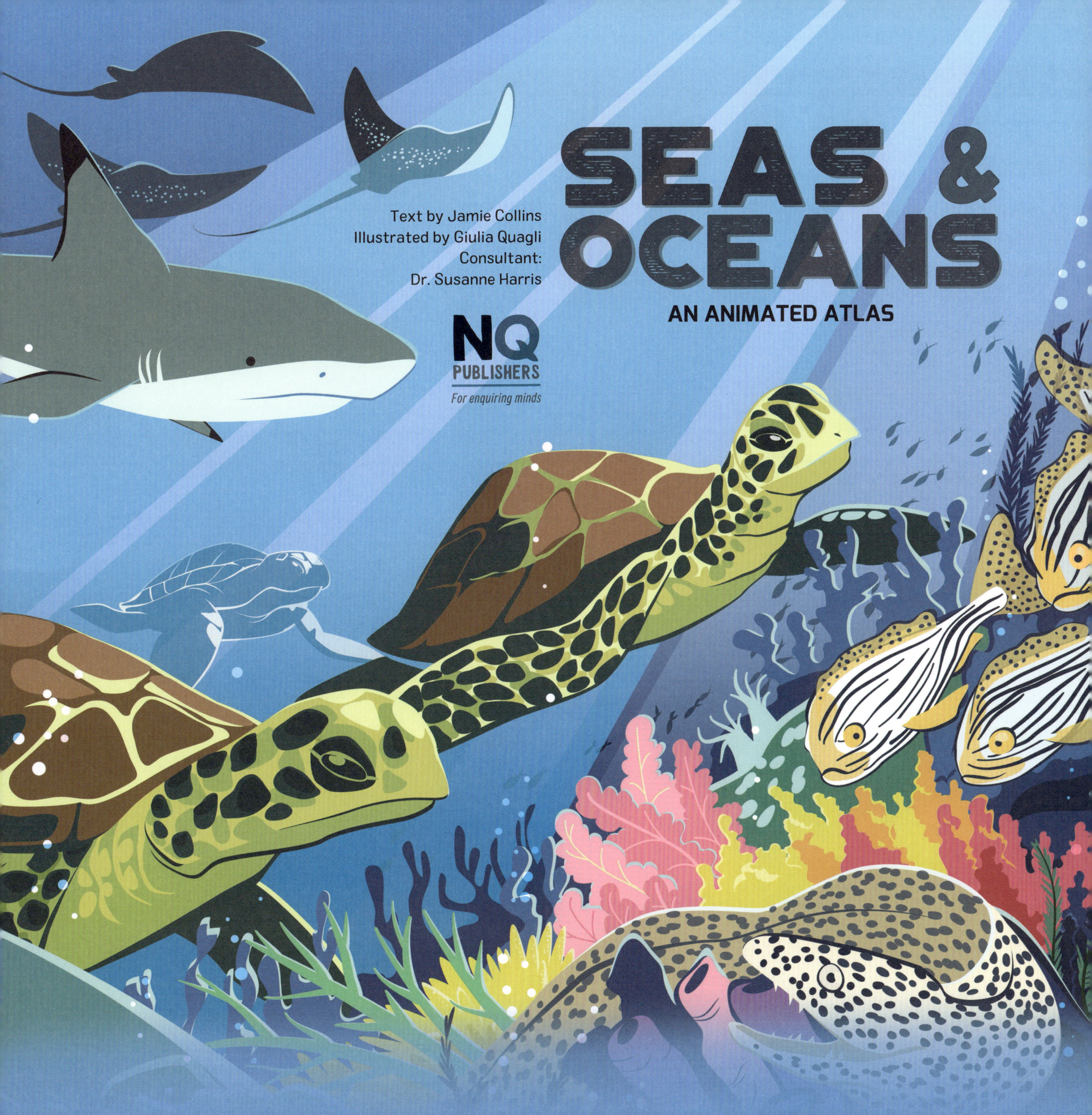

CONTENTS

6-7 OUR BLUE PLANET
The Global Ocean

8-9 THE ARCTIC OCEAN
The Frozen Ocean

16-17 DEEP SEA VENTS
Underwater Wonderlands

18-19 KELP FORESTS
Bustling Ecosystems

20-21 THE GREAT BARRIER REEF
Coral Reefs

10-11 SUMMER FEAST
Life in Cold Northern Waters

12-13 THE PACIFIC OCEAN
The Largest Ocean

14-15 TIDE POOLS
Life on the Rocks

22-23 THE ATLANTIC OCEAN
The Saltiest Ocean

24-25 THE SARGASSO SEA
A Coastless Sea

26-27 THE MEDITERRANEAN SEA
The Most Threatened Sea in the World

28-29	**THE OCEAN DEPTHS** Deep Sea Creatures	**38-39**	**THE SOUTHERN OCEAN** The Youngest Ocean
30-31	**THE INDIAN OCEAN** The Warmest Ocean	**40-41**	**LIFE AMONG THE ICEBERGS** Adapting to the Cold
		42-43	**OCEAN EXPLORATION** Mapping the Oceans

32-33   **WHERE RIVERS MEET THE SEA**
Estuaries, Salt Marshes and Deltas

34-35   **SHALLOW SEAS**
Continental Shelves

36-37   **MANGROVE FORESTS**
Seawater Shrubs and Trees

44-45   **OCEANS IN DANGER**
The Ecology of our Oceans

46-48   **INDEX**

Our Blue Planet

More than 70 per cent of the world is covered by seas and oceans. Earth is the only planet we know of that has large amounts of liquid water on its surface. It is water that makes life on Earth possible. The oceans provide us with air to breathe and food to eat. They regulate climate and weather and provide global transportation routes. Increasingly, ocean winds and tides power turbines that produce clean energy.

LUNGS OF THE PLANET
You may have heard that rainforests are the "lungs of the planet" because they absorb carbon dioxide and give off oxygen. It is true that rainforests do this, but more than half of the oxygen we breathe is produced by microscopic sea creatures called phytoplankton. They also absorb carbon.

From space our planet looks like a swirly blue ball. The swirls are clouds, which are made of icy water. The planet seems blue from afar because seawater absorbs colours like red and yellow, but it reflects blue, which is what we see.

The Arctic Ocean

The Arctic is the smallest and shallowest ocean. It covers the top of our planet, and is surrounded by Europe, Asia and North America. During the winter it is almost completely frozen over, but large parts of the ice melt during the warmer months. Because of global warming, every summer more and more of the ice melts. Scientists fear that soon all the ice will thaw, making life difficult for the people and animals that live here.

ARCTIC OCEAN
the scoop

1. The Arctic Ocean takes its name from the ancient Greek word *arktos* which means "bear."
2. The long cold Arctic winter lasts from September to May.
3. On cloudless dark nights between late August and April you can sometimes see amazing colourful lights dancing across the sky. They are called the northern lights, or aurora borealis.
4. The North Pole is located in the frozen Arctic Ocean.
5. The Arctic Ocean is the least salty of all the oceans.

A giant **humpback whale** breaches the chilly Arctic waves. Whales usually breach when the seas are rough so that they can breathe the air.

Humpback whale

Polar bears

Many **polar bears** spend their entire lives on drifting ice floes. They dive into the sea to hunt fish and seals. As the Arctic sea ice melts, they have less and less space to live.

Polar bear cubs

THE FROZEN OCEAN

Short-tailed shearwaters, also known as muttonbirds or moonbirds, breed on islands around Australia and New Zealand. Every year, several million of them fly 10,500 km (6,500 miles) north to the Bering Sea to feed on krill. An estimated 16 million shearwaters come each year, travelling in flocks that can be 50 km (30 miles) long.

Short-tailed shearwaters

Shearwaters can dive up to 50 metres (160 ft) into the sea to catch the krill. Mackerel, seals, sea lions and whales also join the feeding frenzy.

Shearwaters

Sea lions

Fur seal

Mackerel

Krill

Herrings

Summer Feast

The summer is short in the cold north. When sunlight returns to the Bering Sea in July and August it warms the waters and trillions of fast-growing phytoplankton bloom. They provide food for tiny shrimp-like krill and other small fish, which are the favourite meals of many creatures, including millions of sea birds that travel halfway across the globe to feast on them.

Humpback whales open their giant jaws and leap up out of the water. Their mouths swell with water and krill, then the water is strained away. This is called lunge feeding and it allows them to catch a tonne of krill in just a few hours, enough to keep them going for a whole day.

Humpback whales

The **Bering Sea** lies in the North Pacific. It is home to many whale species, such as the bowhead whale, blue whale, fin whale, sei whale, humpback whale, sperm whale and the rarest of them all, the North Pacific right whale.

TINY LITTLE DRIFTERS
Phytoplankton are tiny plant-like seaweeds that use photosynthesis to create energy from sunlight. They are the basis of the food chain in the oceans. There are many different types — see below.

PACIFIC OCEAN
the scoop

1. The Pacific Ocean is shrinking by about 2.5 cm (1 inch) per year.
2. It was named by the Portuguese explorer Ferdinand Magellan. He called it the *mar pacific*, or "peaceful sea."
3. The edges of the Pacific are encircled by a massive belt of active volcanoes known as the "ring of fire."
4. The Pacific has over 75,000 volcanoes and more than 80 per cent of the world's large earthquakes happen here.
5. It is home to the Great Pacific Garbage Patch. About the size of Texas, it has more plastic waste than any other place on Earth.

The Pacific Ocean

The Pacific covers about one third of our planet and holds almost half of its water. It is bigger than all of the Earth's landmasses combined. The Pacific is not only the largest ocean, it is also the deepest. The Mariana Trench in the northeast is at least 11,000 metres (36,000 ft) deep. If you put Mount Everest into the Mariana Trench, its top would still be covered by 2 km (1.2 miles) of water.

The Pacific has more **islands** than any other ocean. There are about 25,000! Some, like Vanuatu and Hawaii, have active volcanoes and coral reefs, while others such as the Easter Islands, have huge statues left by ancient peoples who once lived here.

Here you can see life on the **Galápagos Islands** which lie 1,000 km (600 miles) off the coast of South America. They are very remote and the animals that live here have evolved in unique ways. They include the world's largest tortoise (the Galápagos tortoise), the only sea-going lizards (marine iguanas), and the sole penguin species that lives north of the equator (the Galápagos penguin).

THE BIRTHPLACE OF ECOLOGY
The Galápagos Islands are the birthplace of the modern science of ecology. This is where Charles Darwin made discoveries that led to his groundbreaking theory of evolution.

Blue-footed booby

Marine iguanas

Marine iguanas are usually browny-black but during the mating season the males become brightly coloured. Ungainly on land, the iguanas bask together in the sun then slip into the waves to feed on seaweed.

THE LARGEST OCEAN

ARCTIC OCEAN

ASIA

Northern fur seal

Giant octopus

Sea otter

NORTH AMERICA

Mahi-mahi

White-sided dolphin

ATLANTIC OCEAN

Frilled shark

NORTH PACIFIC OCEAN

White spotted jellyfish

Lagoon triggerfish

Hawaiian monk seal

Dugong

Galápagos penguin

Pacific sail fish

AUSTRALIA

Sailfin tang

SOUTH AMERICA

Pacific gull

Great frigatebird

SOUTH PACIFIC OCEAN

Tawaki penguin

Killer whale

Sally lightfoot crab

Great white shark

ANTARCTICA

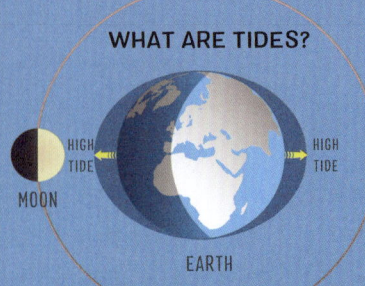

WHAT ARE TIDES?

Tides are the regular rise and fall of sea levels. There are two high tides and two low tides each day. Tides are caused by the gravity of the moon and the sun pulling on the water in our oceans.

Sea birds wait by the rocks until the tide goes out. The creatures in the tide pools have to hide to avoid being eaten.

Sea gulls

Egret

Low tide is the best time to visit a rock pool. Try not to disturb the animals, or capture them.

Sea stars have special sticky feet that stop them from being washed away by the tides.

Hermit crab

Sea lions

Spiny lobster

Bat star

Sea stars

Sea urchins

Red barnacles

Sea anemone

Nudibranchs

Periwinkle

Tide Pools

Tide pools are pockets of seawater that form along rocky sea shores every time the tide goes out. The water gets trapped in hollows between the rocks until the high tide comes wooshing back in. Many creatures live here and they have unique ways of surviving. Some of them, like limpets and mussels, attach themselves to the rocks so that they don't get washed away. Others shelter in cracks or hide under shingle or sand. Some small fish live mostly in the tide pool, but sometimes go out to find more food.

This illustration shows a **tide pool** in California. Tide pools, also known as rock pools, can be found on rocky shorelines all over the world.

Larger animals like **sea lions** and **pelicans** also feed at tide pools. They eat fish and crustaceans such as lobsters and barnacles. They are very happy when a large creature like an octopus gets trapped in a tide pool. They have a feast!

Most tide pools are small but there is plenty of food. The waves roll in full of nutrients and microscopic creatures like plankton. These are eaten by the smallest animals who, in their turn, are eaten by the larger ones.

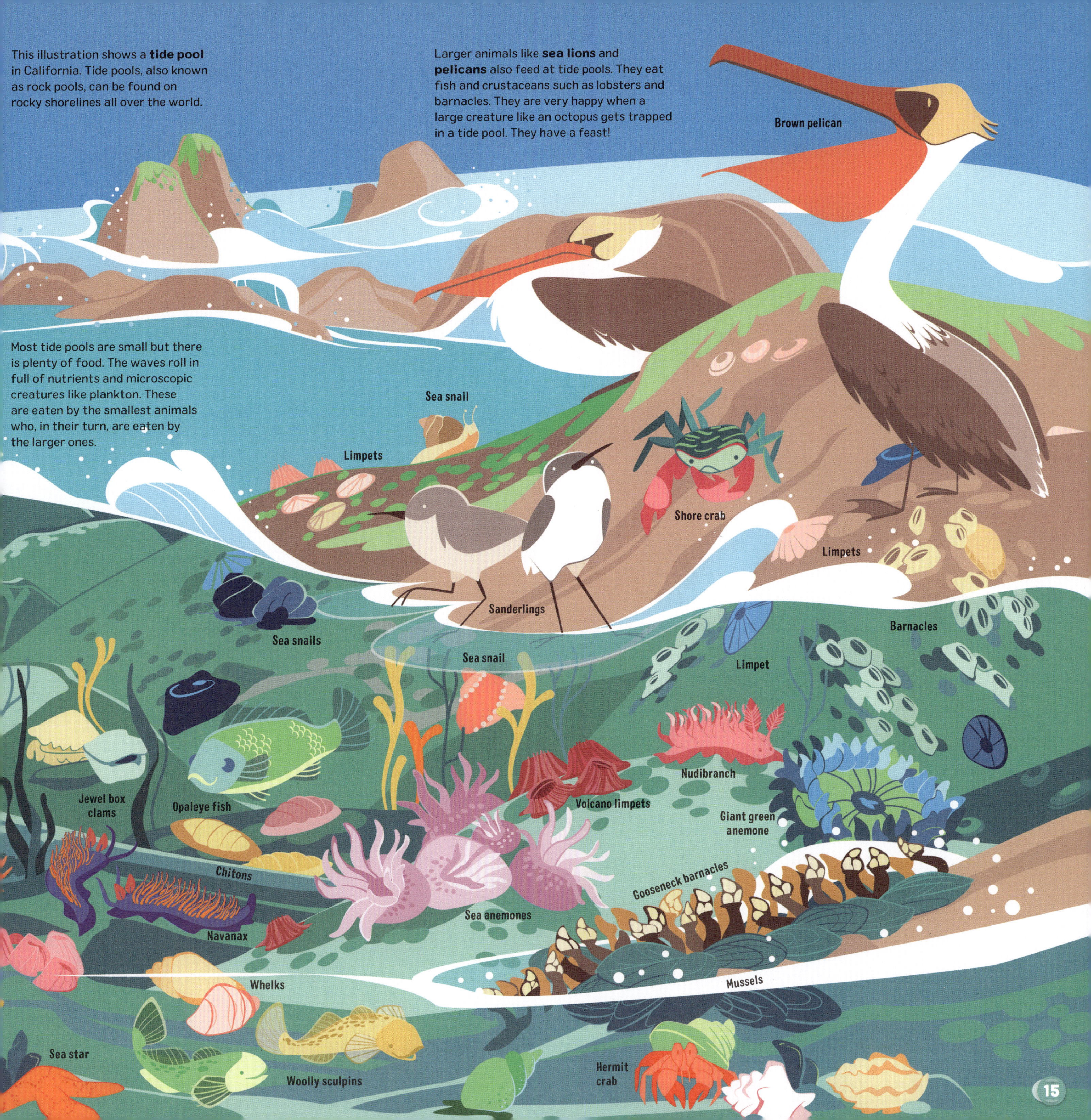

Brown pelican

Sea snail

Limpets

Shore crab

Sanderlings

Limpets

Sea snails

Sea snail

Barnacles

Limpet

Jewel box clams

Opaleye fish

Nudibranch

Volcano limpets

Giant green anemone

Chitons

Gooseneck barnacles

Navanax

Sea anemones

Whelks

Mussels

Sea star

Woolly sculpins

Hermit crab

DEEP SEA VENTS AROUND THE WORLD

The Earth's crust is divided into seven large pieces and many smaller ones. The pieces are called tectonic plates. Almost all deep sea vents occur where the plates meet.

- Deep sea vents

A UNIQUE FOOD CHAIN

All the animals that live around deep sea vents depend on bacteria that feed on the chemicals that come out of the vents. These bacteria form the basis of the food chain. This is different from every other ecosystem on Earth where plants, or plant-like organisms, form the basis of every food chain.

WHERE LIFE BEGAN

Many scientists believe that life on our planet first appeared around deep sea vents. The chemical reactions that occur when alkaline fluids flowing up the vents meet with acidic seawater may have created the first living cells.

Albino octopus

Large black or white "chimneys" often form around the vents. They are made of minerals such as iron, copper and zinc. Some are 180 feet (55 m) tall, or as high as a 12-story building!

Black smoker

Sea dandelion

Shrimp

Sea anemones

Jellyfish

Yeti crabs

Zoarcid fish

Giant tube worms

16 UNDERWATER WONDERLANDS

THE OCEAN FLOOR

Volcano

Continental crust

Oceanic crust

Sea vent

The thin outer layer of our planet is called the crust. When the crust under the ocean meets the crust under the land, it dives underneath. This is how the ocean floor renews itself.

Deep Sea Vents

Deep sea vents are cracks in the ocean floor. Scientists were astonished when they discovered them. Like geysers, they shoot plumes of very hot water into the cold ocean depths. The area around the vents is teeming with life. Many of the plants and animals that live there are unique. There are huge, red-tipped tube worms anchored to the ocean floor, giant clams, furry crabs and ghostly fish with huge eyes. Some scientists think that life on Earth may have begun in the areas around deep sea vents.

Gulper eels have mouths that are much bigger than their bodies. Not only can they eat prey much larger than themselves, they can puff their bodies up to scare away predators.

Gulper eel

Pompeii worm

Giant clams

Vent crab

Pacific viperfish

Left: Giant tube worms are among the strangest creatures in this habitat. Two metres (6 ft) long and as thick as your arm, they have no mouths or stomachs and eat food produced by bacteria that live inside them. These strange creatures never leave their tubes, which protect them from predators and toxic chemicals from the vents.

Kelp Forests

About a quarter of the world's coastlines are lined with huge underwater forests of kelp. Kelps are large brown algae, or seaweeds. There are many different types. The tallest ones, called giant kelps, can tower up to 80 metres (200 ft) high. They can grow 60 cm (2 ft) in a single day, faster than any plant. Kelp forests provide food and shelter for many sea creatures.

KELPS

Kelps look like plants but they are not part of the plant kingdom. They are algae, or seaweeds. Kelps don't have roots, they have holdfasts that anchor them to the seabed. They absorb nutrients from the water and use sunlight to make energy through photosynthesis.

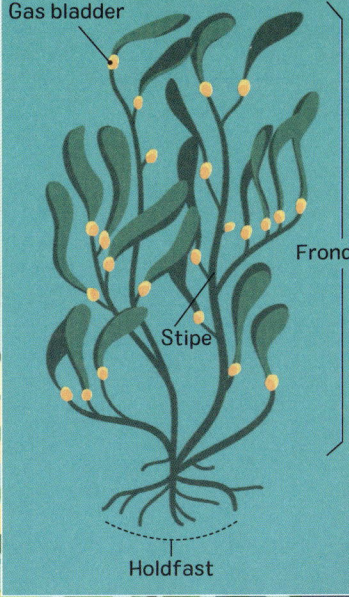

Gas bladder
Frond
Stipe
Holdfast

Torpedo ray

Pacific harbour seal

Wolf eels

Two-spot octopus

Giant sea bass

The **giant sea bass** is the king of the kelp forests that grow along the coast of California. This huge fish weighs more than 250 kg (500 lb), or about as much as seven large dogs!

CORAL REEFS AROUND THE WORLD

Coral reefs form in tropical seas all over the world. The Great Barrier Reef lies off the east coast of Australia.

ENDANGERED REEF

Scientists fear that the Great Barrier Reef is dying, along with many other coral reefs around the world. Much of the damage is caused by global warming as sea temperatures rise above levels that the corals can tolerate.

There are hundreds of different types of **coral** on the Barrier Reef, including hard corals, soft corals, sea pens, blue corals and sea fans.

The **tiger shark** is one of the most dangerous animals on the Barrier Reef. They are quite rare. Reef sharks are much more common.

CROSS SECTION OF A STONY CORAL

Corals are made up of hundreds of tiny creatures called polyps. Each polyp is a sac-like animal with a mouth surrounded by tentacles. Corals attach themselves to rocks and sand in shallow seas and gradually grow into large structures, called reefs.

- Tentacle
- Mouth
- Stomach

Labels: Coral, Minke whale, Sponges, Emperor angelfish, Parrot fish, Dolphins, Butterfly fish, Reef shark, Tiger shark, Elephant ear sponge, Sponges, Girdled angelfish, Clown triggerfish, Biscuit sea star, Crown-of-thorns sea star

20 CORAL REEFS

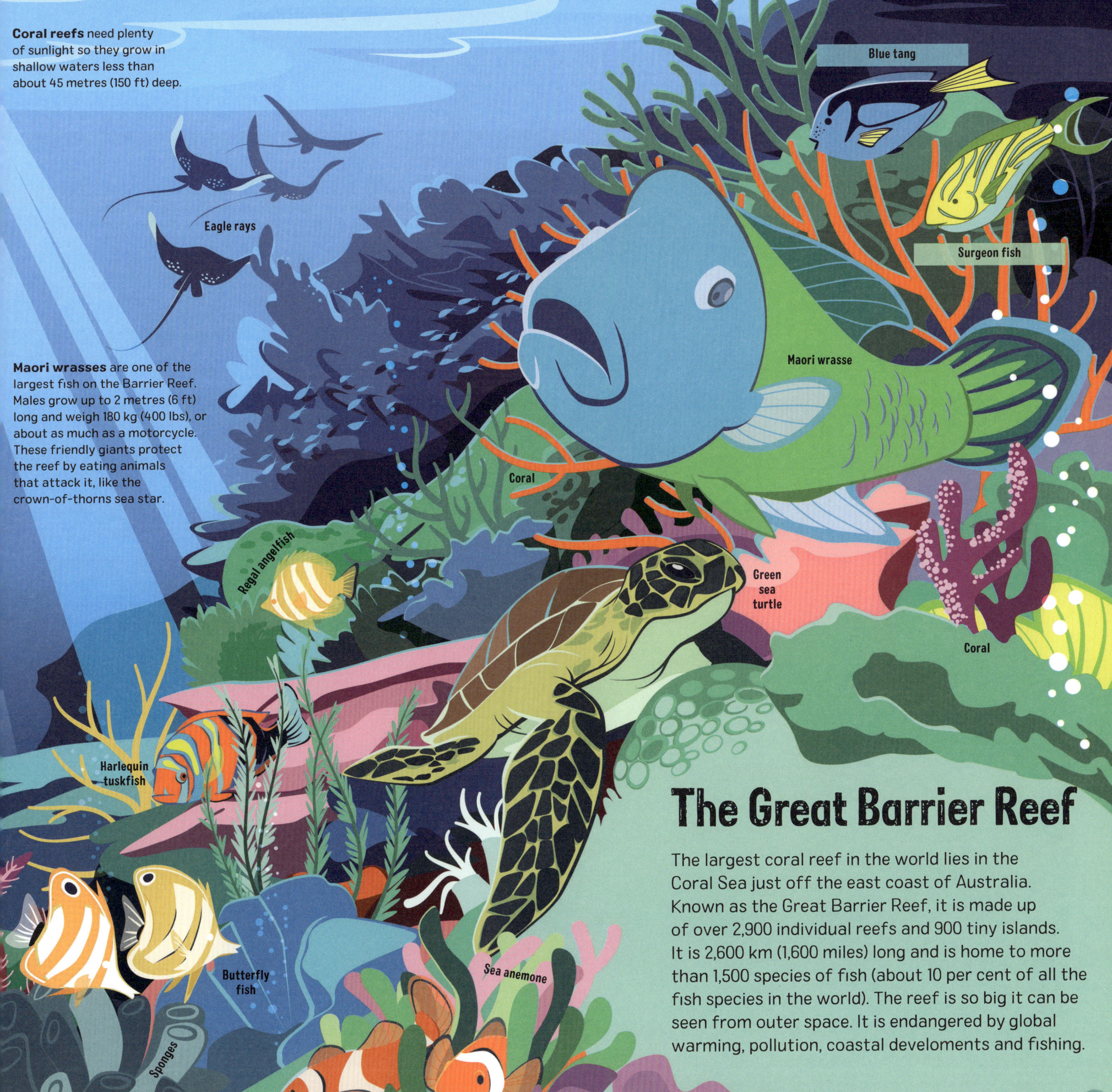

Coral reefs need plenty of sunlight so they grow in shallow waters less than about 45 metres (150 ft) deep.

Maori wrasses are one of the largest fish on the Barrier Reef. Males grow up to 2 metres (6 ft) long and weigh 180 kg (400 lbs), or about as much as a motorcycle. These friendly giants protect the reef by eating animals that attack it, like the crown-of-thorns sea star.

The Great Barrier Reef

The largest coral reef in the world lies in the Coral Sea just off the east coast of Australia. Known as the Great Barrier Reef, it is made up of over 2,900 individual reefs and 900 tiny islands. It is 2,600 km (1,600 miles) long and is home to more than 1,500 species of fish (about 10 per cent of all the fish species in the world). The reef is so big it can be seen from outer space. It is endangered by global warming, pollution, coastal develoments and fishing.

The Atlantic Ocean

The Atlantic covers about one fifth of the planet and is the second largest ocean, after the Pacific. It is shaped like a huge letter "S" and runs all the way from the Arctic Ocean in the north to the Southern Ocean in the south. The Atlantic was formed about 150 million years ago in the Jurassic Period, when the supercontinent Pangaea split in two. It has rugged coastlines and includes many bays, gulfs and seas.

ATLANTIC OCEAN
the scoop

1. The Atlantic is growing wider by about 10 cm (4 in) a year. It grows at about the same rate as your fingernails.
2. It is the saltiest ocean.
3. It has the highest tides in the world — at the Bay of Fundy, in Canada.
4. The mid-Atlantic Ridge is part of the world's longest mountain chain. It runs 16,000 km (10,000 miles) from Iceland to the southern tip of Africa.
5. The "unsinkable" Titanic sank in the North Atlantic in April 1912 three hours after hitting an iceberg.

Great black-backed gull

Narwhals live in the icy waters of the Arctic and North Atlantic oceans. They have a long "tooth" on their noses and are sometimes called the unicorns of the sea.

Narwhals

Puffins

Puffins live in large colonies on cliffs high above the Arctic and North Atlantic oceans. These skillful fliers have short wings that work equally well underwater as they hunt for fish. Their big beaks turn bright orange in the breeding season.

THE SALTIEST OCEAN

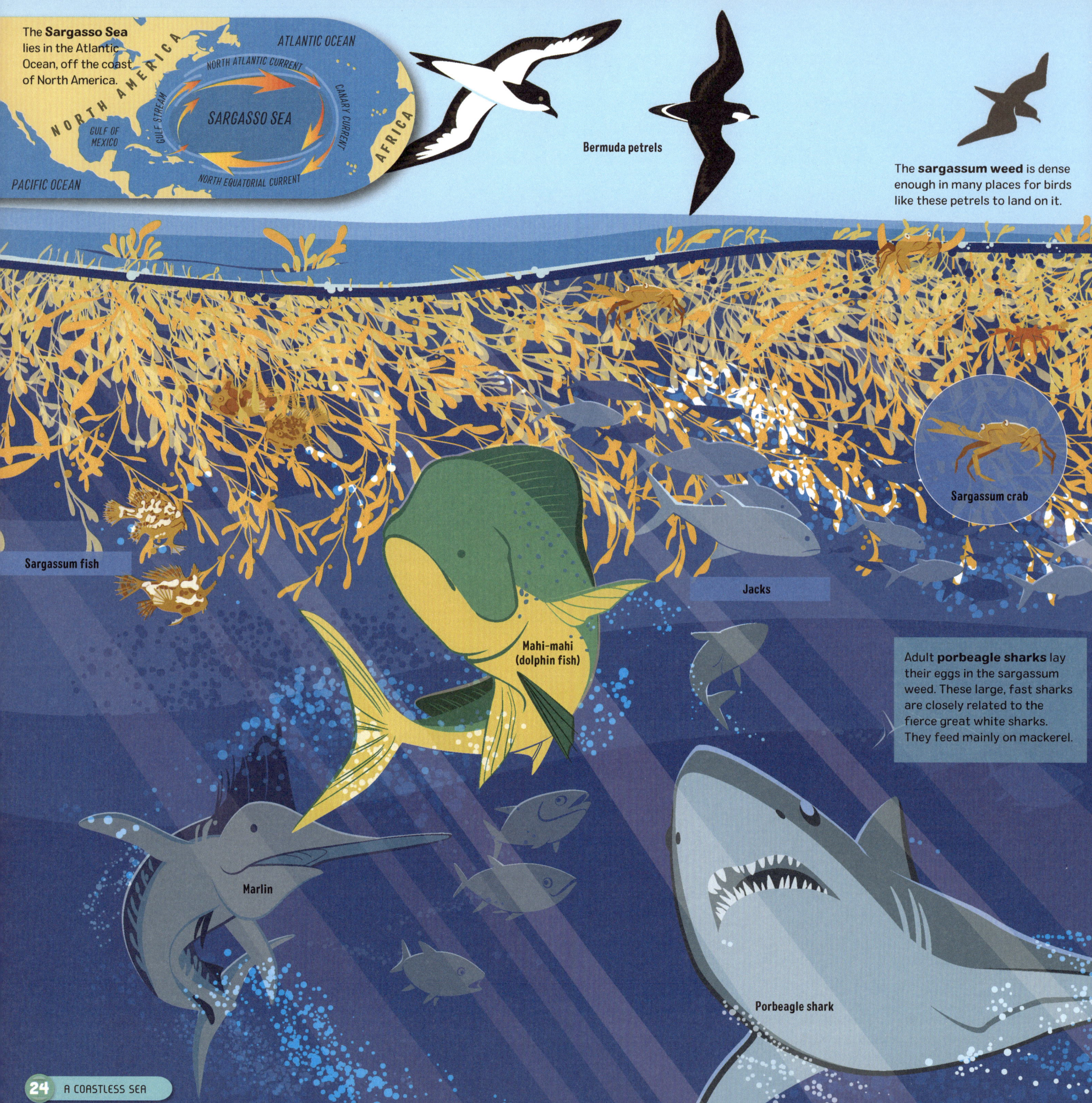

Eels from America and Europe spawn in the Sargasso Sea. European eels swim about 6,500 km (4,000 miles) to the Sargasso where the females lay their eggs. The baby eels hatch then take about 300 days to drift back to Europe. They live in rivers for several years before returning to the Sargasso to lay their own eggs and die.

Willets

The **Sargasso Sea** is a giant nursery for many young creatures, but especially for baby sea turtles who would not survive in the open sea without the sargassum weed.

Baby sea turtles

Adult eel

Young eel

Triggerfish

Fishing net

Green sea turtle

This green sea turtle is caught up in an old fishing net.

Plastic

POLLUTION
The Sargasso is badly polluted with plastic, which gets trapped in the gyre (spiral) created by the ocean currents. The plastic gets caught in the sargassum weed, making it very hard to clean up. The animals that live in the sargassum weed often eat the toxic plastic or get trapped by it.

The Sargasso Sea

The Sargasso is the only sea in the world that has no coastlines. Instead of land, its borders are four large ocean currents. The sea is named for the thick mat of yellow sargassum weed on its surface which provides food and shelter for many creatures. Eels, marlin, porbeagle sharks and mahi-mahi all spawn here. Their young are safe among the weeds until they can take care of themselves.

25

OVERFISHING

The Mediterranean is the most overfished sea in the world and many fish stocks are dying out. Some fishing boats drag nets along the sea floor behind them. These can wipe out entire ecosystems and kill animals like sea turtles. Bottom trawling is banned in some areas.

HOT SPOT

The Mediterranean is a hotspot for plant and animal life. Many of the animals living here don't exist anywhere else. Sadly, most of them are in danger of dying out because of overfishing, pollution, chemicals and invasive species.

FRANCE

Fishing boat

Flamingos

Gulls
Striped dolphin
Spiny lobster
Whales
Mussels
Parrot fish
SICILY
ADRIATIC S
ITALY
Red sea st
SARDINIA
MEDITERRANEAN SEA
SICILY

Flamingos are native to many parts of the Mediterranean.

PORTUGAL
SPAIN

The Atlantic meets the Mediterranean at the **Strait of Gibraltar**. The salty, heavier waters of the Mediterranean flow out along the sea floor while the lighter Atlantic seawaters flow in near the surface.

Seahorse
Fin whale

Eight different species of **whales** and **dolphins** live in the Mediterranean, including the **fin whale**, which is the second-largest animal on Earth. (The blue whale is the biggest).

Strait of Gibraltar
Harbour porpoise

MOROCCO
ALGERIA
TUNISIA

ATLANTIC OCEAN

The Mediterranean Sea

The Mediterranean Sea is sometimes considered to be part of the Atlantic Ocean, but it is really a separate — and very special — sea. It is almost entirely surrounded by land, and only connected to the Atlantic by the narrow Strait of Gibraltar between Spain and Morocco. The Black Sea lies further east and is also almost landlocked. Both seas have weaker tides and are much saltier than the open oceans.

With only a few hundred individuals left in the wild, the gentle **monk seal** is among the rarest creatures on Earth. Many animals in the Mediterranean Sea are endangered.

Mediterranean monk seals

MOST THREATENED SEA IN THE WORLD

THE BLACK SEA

Many rivers flow into the Black Sea, making it rich enough in sediment and nutrients to support a wide range of marine life. Water flows out of the Black Sea into the Mediterranean through the Bosphorus Strait.

The **Beluga sturgeon** is one of the largest fish in the world. Beluga caviar (roe) is a great delicacy, and very expensive!

Loggerhead and **green sea turtles** both breed in the Mediterranean.

The **Suez Canal** links the Red Sea with the Mediterranean. Since the canal opened in 1869, plants and animals from the Indian Ocean have come through into the Mediterranean Sea. Some of them pose a threat to local plants and animals; they are known as invasive species.

Labels on map: Beluga sturgeon, Spider crab, White-spotted octopus, Devilfish, Ornate wrasse, Loggerhead turtle, Bluefin tuna, Bigfin reef squid, Dusky spinefoot, Cornetfish, Puffer fish, Grape sand moss, Red scorpion fish

Places: UKRAINE, RUSSIA, GEORGIA, ROMANIA, BULGARIA, BLACK SEA, Bosphorus Strait, TURKEY, MONTENEGRO, SERBIA, ALBANIA, GREECE, AEGEAN SEA, IONIAN SEA, CRETE, CYPRUS, LIBYA, EGYPT, Suez Canal, GULF OF SUEZ, GULF OF AQABA, ISRAEL, JORDAN, SAUDI ARABIA, IRAQ

27

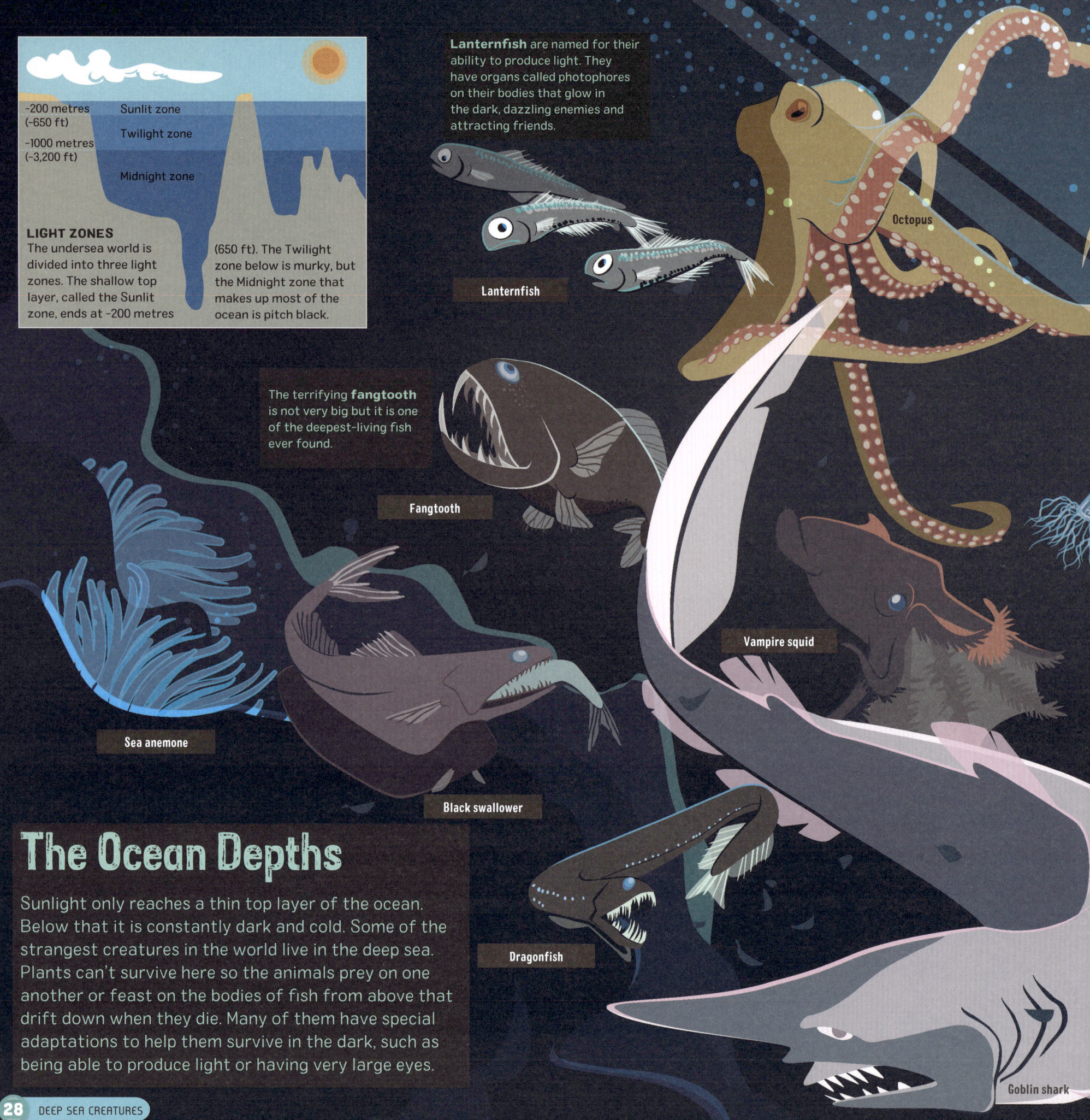

LIGHT ZONES
The undersea world is divided into three light zones. The shallow top layer, called the Sunlit zone, ends at -200 metres (650 ft). The Twilight zone below is murky, but the Midnight zone that makes up most of the ocean is pitch black.

Lanternfish are named for their ability to produce light. They have organs called photophores on their bodies that glow in the dark, dazzling enemies and attracting friends.

The terrifying **fangtooth** is not very big but it is one of the deepest-living fish ever found.

The Ocean Depths

Sunlight only reaches a thin top layer of the ocean. Below that it is constantly dark and cold. Some of the strangest creatures in the world live in the deep sea. Plants can't survive here so the animals prey on one another or feast on the bodies of fish from above that drift down when they die. Many of them have special adaptations to help them survive in the dark, such as being able to produce light or having very large eyes.

28 DEEP SEA CREATURES

INDIAN OCEAN
the scoop
1. Sea levels are rising faster in the northern Indian Ocean than anywhere else in the world.
2. The Indian Ocean has less marine life than other oceans.
3. It has the lowest oxygen content of all the oceans.
4. There is a "lost continent" under the island of Mauritius.
5. The Indian Ocean has oil deposits that account for 40 per cent of world production.

The Indian Ocean

The Indian Ocean covers slightly less than 20 per cent of the Earth's surface and is the third largest ocean. It is the warmest of all the oceans because so much of it lies close to the equator. It is also warming faster than the other oceans because of El Niño and global warming.

Spotted eagle rays

Hawksbill sea turtles live around coral reefs, but also make long journeys in the open sea. They feed mainly on sea sponges. These turtles have beautiful shells. They are almost extinct because people use the shells to make tortoiseshell ornaments.

Black-tipped reef shark

Oriental sweetlips

Hawksbill sea turtles

Moray eel

Moray eels look scarey but they are not very aggressive. They have two sets of jaws, one for grabbing the fish they feed on and another to pull them down their throats.

30 THE WARMEST OCEAN

WORLD'S BIGGEST DELTAS

Here you can see 18 of the largest deltas in the world.

● River deltas

Where Rivers Meet the Sea

Rivers collect rainwater and melted snow from the land and carry them to the ocean. Where rivers meet the sea, they form estuaries and deltas, often lined with salt marshes. These special wetland environments are teeming with wildlife and plants. A lot of people also live in these fertile regions and many of the world's largest cities are located at river mouths.

The **water** in estuaries and salt marshes is brackish, which means it is saltier than freshwater but not as salty as seawater.

THE MEKONG RIVER DELTA

The illustration on these pages shows the Mekong River Delta, in Vietnam. It covers 40,000 sq/km (15,500 square miles) and is home to more than 1,000 animal species. Many new types of plants, fish, lizards and mammals have been discovered here, and the area is known as a biological hot spot.

Great egret

Asian golden weaver

River dolphins

Giant stingray

Mekong giant catfish

ESTUARIES, SALT MARSHES & DELTAS

The Mekong Delta is also home to 22 million people. Wildlife suffers as the human population grows, taking up land to grow rice and farm. These people are exposed to flooding and could lose their homes as sea levels rise.

HOW DELTAS FORM
Deltas form when rivers carrying mud and sediment drop them near the sea. The sediment builds up, splitting the river into channels as extra land forms. Deltas are often very fertile and are intensively farmed.

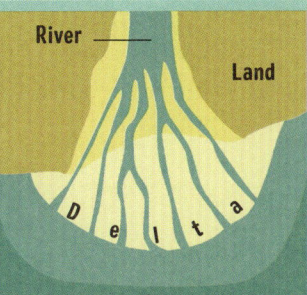

Many endangered species live in the Mekong Delta, including the giant catfish and Irrawaddy dolphins.

Sarus crane

Lesser adjutant

Saola

Oriental darter

Pond heron

Water monitor

Bengal florican

Fanged frog

Leopard gecko

Irrawaddy dolphin

33

CONTINENTAL SHELF

A continental shelf is the edge of a continent that lies under the sea. It slopes away gently from the land, usually for about 65 km (40 miles), but it can be much shorter or longer.

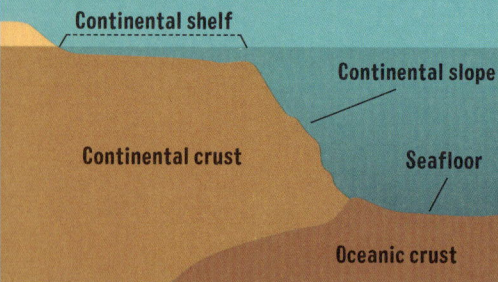

Shallow Seas

The shallow seas that surround the continents make up less than ten per cent of the oceans, but this is where most marine creatures live. The water is warm and filled with nutrients. Plants and seaweeds have plenty of sunlight to produce energy, ensuring that there is food for all.

These coastal waters are teeming with fish and about 90 per cent of fishing and fish farming happens here.

Royal angelfish

Grey reef shark

Devilfish

Pharaoh cuttlefish

Moray eels

Bluefin trevally

Seahorse

SEAGRASS

Seagrass is the only true plant that grows at sea. There are many different types but they all grow in shallow seas because they need sunlight to carry out photosynthesis. Seagrass has roots, but is a rhizome, which means that the plants are joined together by an underground stem.

Indian mackerel

Dugongs are large mammals that live in the warm coastal waters of the Indian and Pacific oceans. They are closely related to manatees.

Green sea turtle

Sea star

Dugongs

Golden trevally

Conch

UNDERWATER MEADOWS

In some places, seagrasses grow in vast underwater meadows. Dugongs are often called sea cows because they feed in these meadows. Many other animals, including green sea turtles, feed on seagrass.

35

MANGROVE FORESTS AROUND THE WORLD

Mangrove forests are shrinking fast. Almost 35 per cent have already been lost.

■ Mangrove forests

Great egrets

Spotted deer

Fishing cat

Fish owl

Mangrove forests act as **nurseries** for a large number of baby animals, providing them with food and shelter.

Irrawaddy dolphins

Paira chandra fish

The **sawfish** is one of the largest fishes in the world. It belongs to the ray family and grows to 7.6 metres (25 ft) in length. Its long nose is lined with sharp teeth.

BUSY ECOSYSTEMS

Mangrove forests are busy. They are home to a large number of small fish, shrimp, crabs, mussels, oysters and barnacles, as well as many larger animals that eat them.

Sawfish

Fiddler crab

Mangrove Forests

Mangrove trees grow along the coasts of tropical seas all over the world. They crowd together in forests, thriving in the infertile mud flats and sandy soils along the shoreline. Their tangled roots and branches create a unique environment and they are teeming with life. Mangrove forests stop the coasts from eroding and form a barrier that protects animals and people from tsunamis and storm surges.

The largest mangrove forests grow in India, in the delta of three rivers that flow into the Bay of Bengal. The region is known as the **Sunderbans**. Here you can see some of the animals that live there.

Bengal tiger

Rhesus monkeys

Brown-winged kingfishers

Fiddler crab

Mudskippers

Saltwater crocodile

MANGROVE TREES

There are many different species of mangrove trees but they are all quite similar. Their roots can be seen above ground and they get oxygen from the air. Mangrove trees can survive in salty water because their roots filter out the salt and discard it.

Roots

Water

Soil

The Southern Ocean

SOUTHERN OCEAN
the scoop
1. The Southern Ocean covers six per cent of the Earth's surface.
2. The deepest point in the Southern Ocean is 7,235 metres (23,737 ft) at the South Sandwich Trench.
3. The world's biggest wave was recorded here in 2018. It was 23.8 metres (92.8 ft) tall.
4. Sailors named the latitudes in the Southern Ocean for their winds: The Roaring Forties (40°S), the Furious Fifties (50°S) and the Screaming Sixties (60°S).
5. No one lives permanently in the Southern Ocean.

The Southern Ocean is one of the coldest, windiest and most remote places on Earth. It is the fourth largest ocean and because it formed "just" 30 million years ago, it is also the youngest ocean. During the winter, half of this wild, remote ocean is frozen solid and its waters are scattered with icebergs all year round. Despite the harsh conditions, many animals make their homes here.

Wandering albatross

The **wandering albatross** has the largest wingspan of any bird. It spends its whole life soaring above the Southern Ocean, only landing to breed.

Emperor penguins with their chicks

Hourglass dolphins

Emperor penguins are the largest of the 17 penguin species. They spend all their time on the Antarctic ice sheets, often huddling together for warmth.

There are fewer fish species here than in the other oceans. Some, such as **icefish**, have antifreeze proteins in their blood, so that the icy water doesn't kill them.

Gentoo penguin

Macaroni penguins

Killer whale

Leopard seal

Gentoo penguin

Life Among the Icebergs

The Southern Ocean has strong currents and upwellings that are rich in microscopic phytoplankton and krill. These tiny creatures are the basis of the food chain. Even the giant blue whale feeds on krill, and eats about 40 million of them every day! The ice sheets around the continent of Antarctica calve (produce) thousands of icebergs every year. Some of the icebergs are more than 100 km (62 miles) long and can take ten years to melt.

Gentoo penguin

Killer whale

Crabeater seal

40 ADAPTING TO THE COLD

Southern Ocean animals have special adaptations to help stay warm. Penguins have thick wind and waterproof feathers. Whales and seals have layers of blubber (fat) under their skins.

Kelp gull

Antarctic fur seal

Antarctic flying squid

Colossal squid

Antarctic toothfish

Blackfin icefish

The **colossal squid** can weigh up to 700 kg (1,500 lbs). It has the largest eyes of any known animal. They measure up to 40 cm (16 in) wide (as big as a very large dinner plate!)

Jellyfish

Blue whale

THE LARGEST ANIMALS
Blue whales are the largest animals that have ever lived. Here you can compare their size with a city bus. They are more than twice as long. Colossal squid are also very large.

City bus

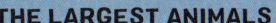

0   100 feet (30 m)

Blue whale

Colossal squid

Krill look like tiny shrimps. They feed on even smaller organisms, called phytoplankton.

Krill

41

SHIPWRECKS

According to some estimates, there are more than three million shipwrecks lying on the ocean floor. The oldest date back more than 10,000 years, while the most recent are from the 21st century. Only about one per cent of wrecks have been recovered.

In 1718, a famous pirate ship called *Queen Anne's Revenge* ran aground off the coast of North Carolina. She was the flagship of the notorious pirate, Blackbeard, aka Edward Thatch. The wreck was discovered in 1996. It took marine archaeologists more than a decade to recover the contents of the ship.

WRECKS AS HOMES FOR MARINE CREATURES

Shipwrecks become a part of the marine environment almost as soon as they come to rest on the seafloor. Wrecks provide an excellent habitat for sea creatures and they are soon part of a thriving ecosystem. The wreck acts like a reef, providing shelter for a variety of fish and crustaceans.

Ocean Exploration

It is often said that we know more about the Moon or Mars than we do about the oceans on our own planet. Only a small part of the ocean floor has been mapped, and not in a very detailed way. It is difficult to map the sea floor because the oceans are deep, dark, huge and often very remote. Scientists from around the world have united to overcome this lack of knowledge.

It is easier to explore shallow seas because divers can use conventional diving gear and oxygen tanks. Scuba divers can go to about 30 metres (100 ft). This is ideal for exploring coral reefs and shallow coastal waters.

Scuba diver

Coral

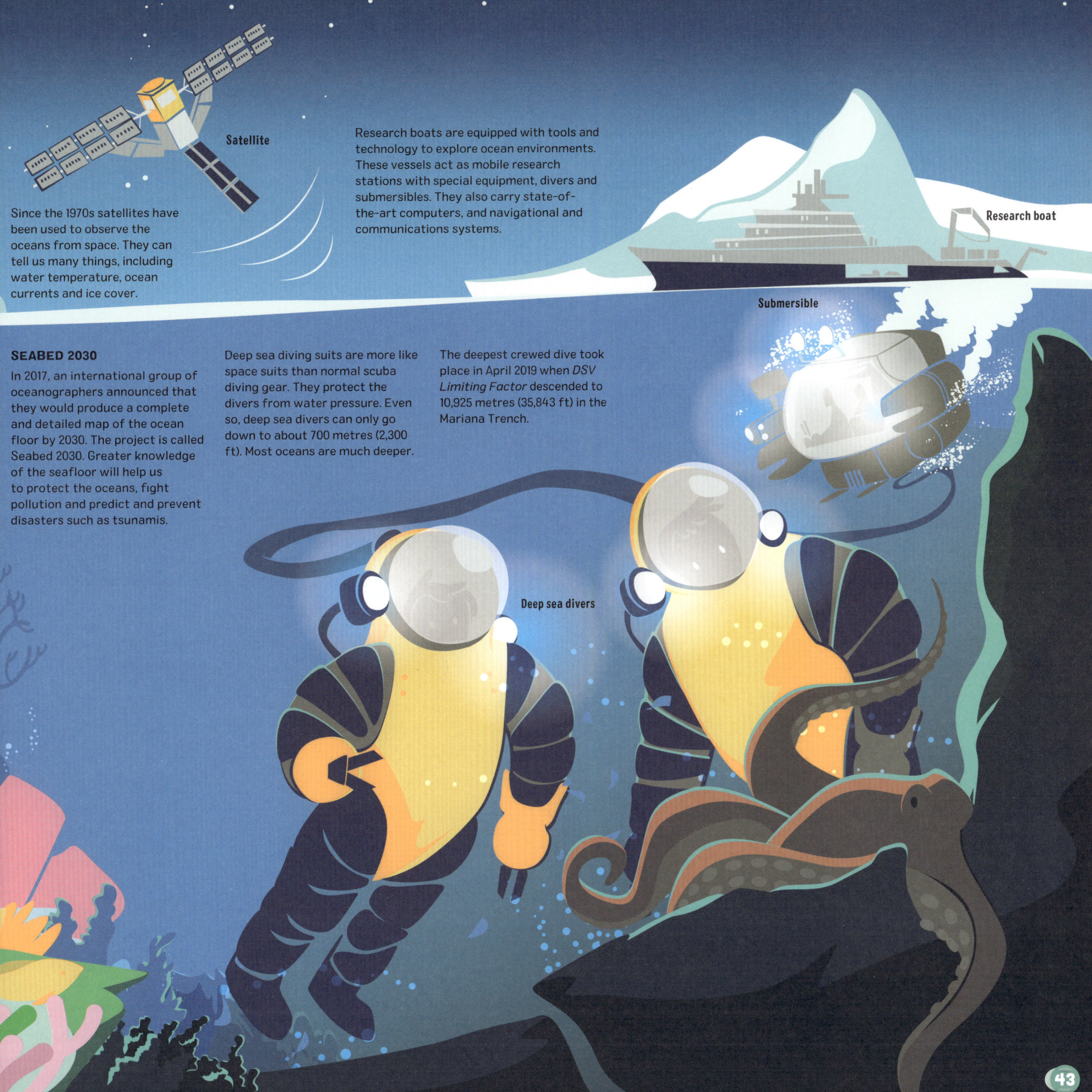

Since the 1970s satellites have been used to observe the oceans from space. They can tell us many things, including water temperature, ocean currents and ice cover.

Satellite

Research boats are equipped with tools and technology to explore ocean environments. These vessels act as mobile research stations with special equipment, divers and submersibles. They also carry state-of-the-art computers, and navigational and communications systems.

Research boat

Submersible

SEABED 2030

In 2017, an international group of oceanographers announced that they would produce a complete and detailed map of the ocean floor by 2030. The project is called Seabed 2030. Greater knowledge of the seafloor will help us to protect the oceans, fight pollution and predict and prevent disasters such as tsunamis.

Deep sea diving suits are more like space suits than normal scuba diving gear. They protect the divers from water pressure. Even so, deep sea divers can only go down to about 700 metres (2,300 ft). Most oceans are much deeper.

The deepest crewed dive took place in April 2019 when *DSV Limiting Factor* descended to 10,925 metres (35,843 ft) in the Mariana Trench.

Deep sea divers

Oceans in Danger

Our oceans face a range of threats, from global warming and pollution to overfishing. We used to think that the oceans were so vast that they would absorb everything we dumped into them. Scientists now know that keeping our oceans healthy is essential for the survival of life as we know it. To achieve this, we need to reduce carbon emissions and reconsider the way we live so that we do not endanger the future of the oceans, and the planet!

Walruses live in the northern oceans and the Arctic. They need sea ice to feed and rest on. Global warming is destroying their habitat.

GLOBAL WARMING
The world is getting warmer because human activities such as industry release greenhouse gases into the atmosphere. In the last 100 years the average global temperature has risen by 1.8°F (1.°C). That might not sound like much, but it is enough to melt sea ice and change the planet's climate.

Melting sea ice causes sea levels to rise. People who live in coastal areas will be flooded and left homeless unless we stop global warming.

Oil spills from offshore platforms and tankers are disastrous for marine habitats. Sea animals swallow the oil while trying to clean themselves and are poisoned. The oil also destroys their feathers and fur and they die of cold.

TRASHING THE OCEANS
Rivers draining into the oceans are polluted with chemicals from factories and farms, and untreated sewage. They also carry millions of plastic bags. The plastic doesn't go away; it accumulates in gigantic gyres in the middle of the oceans, where it traps and is eaten by marine animals.

Walrus

ATLANTIC OCEAN

EUROPE

AFRICA

ASIA

INDIAN OCEAN

AUSTRALIA

Steller's sea eagle

Napoleon wrasse

Amsterdam albatross

THE ECOLOGY OF OUR OCEANS

ARCTIC OCEAN

Chinook salmon

NORTH AMERICA

Acid seawater kills off corals and sea creatures with shells, like oysters and clams.

SUSTAINABLE FISHING

Sustainable fishing means leaving enough fish in the seas so that stocks can replenish. It also means respecting the marine environment and the people make a living from fishing. Overfishing damages habitats and can wipe out species. Fish provide food and work for billions of people.

ACID SEAS

The oceans absorb carbon dioxide and they have helped to slow global warming. But too much carbon dioxide has made the seawater more acidic than many plants and animals can tolerate.

ATLANTIC OCEAN

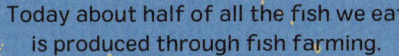
Today about half of all the fish we eat is produced through fish farming.

Vaquita porpoise

SOUTH AMERICA

Manatee

Sea turtles

Plastic is a manmade product that decomposes very slowly. A foam plastic cup takes about 50 years to decay, while a disposable nappy takes more than 400 years. About ten per cent of all the plastic made ends up in the sea.

OCEAN CLEANUP

Plastic waste and other debris get caught in ocean gyres (huge spirals of water made by currents and winds), creating vast garbage patches. Ecologists are trying to clean up the plastic, but it is a huge job.

PACIFIC OCEAN

Hector's Dolphin

Hooded seal

SOUTHERN OCEAN

45

Index

A
Adélie penguin 39
African penguin 31
albino octopus 16
albatross
  -Amsterdam albatross 44
  -Indian yellow-nosed albatross 31
  -royal albatross 7
  -wandering albatross 38
anglerfish 29
Antarctic flying squid 41
Antarctic fur seal 41
Antarctic petrel 39
Antarctic sea spider 39
Antarctic shag 39
Antarctic toothfish 39, 41
Arctic flounder 9
Arctic octopus 9
Arctic tern 9, 39
Asian golden weaver 32
Atlantic cod 9
Atlantic white-sided dolphin 23

B
bald eagle 9
barnacles 15
barracuda 6
bat star 14
beluga 9
beluga sturgeon 27
Bengal florican 33
Bengal tiger 37
Bermuda petrels 24
bigfin reef squid 27
biscuit sea star 20
black smoker 16
black swallower 28
black-tipped reef shark 30
blackfin icefish 41
blue shark 7
blue tang 21
blue whale 6, 41
blue-footed booby 12
blue-ringed octopus 6
bluefin trevally 34
bluefin tuna 23, 27
bottlenose dolphin 31, 33
bottlenose whale 39
bowhead whale 9
brown pelican 15
brown-winged kingfishers 37
butterfly fish 2, 21

C
cabezon 18
California sheephead 18
Cape fur seal 23
cauliflower jellyfish 31
chinook salmon 9, 45
chinstrap penguin 39
chitons 15
clown fish 21
clown triggerfish 20
coconut crab 31
colossal squid 39, 41
Commerson's dolphin 7, 23
conch 35
coral 20, 21, 42
cornetfish 27
crabeater seal 39, 40
crocodile icefish 39
crown-of-thorns sea star 20

D
deep sea divers 43
delta 33
devilfish 27, 34
dolphins 20
  -Atlantic white-sided dolphin 23
  -bottlenose dolphin 31
  -Commerson's dolphin 7, 23
  -dusky dolphin 39
  -Hector's dolphin 45
  -hourglass dolphins 38
  -Indian ocean humpback dolphin 31
  -Irrawaddy dolphin 33, 36
  -river dolphins 32
  -striped dolphin 26
  -white-sided dolphin 13
dragonfish 28
dugong 13, 35
dusky dolphin 39
dusky spinefoot 27

E
eagle rays 21
eel 25
  -gulper eel 17
  -moray eel 30, 34
egret 14
elephant ear sponge 20
emperor angelfish 20
emperor penguins 38

F
fanged frog 33
fangtooth 28
fiddler crab 36, 37
fin whale 26
fish owl 36
fishing 26
fishing cat 36
flamingos 26
football fish 29
frilled shark 13, 29
fur seal 10

G
Galápagos penguin 13
gentoo penguin 40
giant clam 17, 31
giant green sea anemone 15, 18
giant isopod 29
giant octopus 13
giant sea bass 19
giant spider crab 29
giant stingray 32
giant travelly 31
giant tube worms 16
girdled angelfish 20
goblin shark 28
golden trevally 35
gooseneck barnacles 15

grape sand moss 27
great black-backed
  gull 22
great egret 32, 36
great frigatebird 13
great white shark 13
green sea turtle 21,
  25, 35
Greenland shark 9
grey reef shark 34
grey seal 23
gulls 14, 26
-great black-backed
  gull 22
-ivory gulls 9
-kelp gull 41
-Pacific gull 13
gulper eel 17

H
hammerhead shark 31
harbour porpoise 26
harlequin tuskfish 21
harp seal 9
Hawaiian monk seal 13
Hawksbill sea turtle 30
Hector's dolphin 45
hermit crab 14, 15
herrings 10
hooded seal 45
hourglass dolphins 38
humpback whale 8, 11
I
immortal jellyfish 29
Indian mackerel 35
Indian ocean humpback
  dolphin 31

Indian yellow-nosed
  albatross 31
Irrawaddy dolphins 36
island rail 23
ivory gulls 9

J
jacks 24
jellyfish 16, 39, 41
jewel box clams 15

K
kelp gull 41
killer whale 13, 40
king eider 9
king penguin 39
krill 10, 39, 41

L
lagoon triggerfish 13
lanternfish 28
leatherback turtle 23
lemon shark 23
leopard gecko 33
leopard seal 40
leopard shark 18
lesser adjutant 33
limpet 15
lionfish 31
lobster 23
loggerhead turtle 27
M
macaroni penguins 40
mackerel 10
magellanic penguin 23
mahi-mahi (dolphin
  fish) 13, 24

manatee 23, 45
mandarin fish 31
mantis shrimp 31
Maori wrasse 21
marine iguanas 12
marlin 24
masked booby 23
Mediterranean monk
  seal 23, 26
Mekong giant catfish 32
minke whale 20
moray eel 30, 34
mudskipper 23, 37
mussels 15, 26

N
Napoleon wrasse 44
narwhal 9, 22
navanax 15
Northern fur seal 13
nudibranch 14, 15, 18

O
oceanic crust 34
octopus 28, 31
opaleye fish 15
oriental darter 33
oriental sweetlips 30
ornate wrasse 27
P
Pacific gull 13
Pacific sail fish 13
Pacific sea nettle 7
Pacific viperfish 17
paira chandra fish 36
parrot fish 20, 26
penguin

-Adélie penguin 39
-African penguin 31
-chinstrap penguin 39
-emperor penguins 38
-Galápagos penguin 13
-gentoo penguin 40
-king penguin 39
-macaroni penguins 40
-magellanic penguin 23
-rockhopper penguin 7
-Tawaki penguin 13
periwinkle 14
pharaoh cuttlefish 34
phytoplankton 31
Picasso triggerfish 31
plastic 25
polar bear 6, 8, 9
polar cod 9
Pompeii worm 17
pond heron 33
porbeagle shark 24
puffer fish 27, 31
puffins 22

R
rainbow parrotfish 7
red barnacles 14
red scorpion fish 27
red sea star 26
reef shark 20
regal angelfish 21, 31
rhesus monkeys 37
ribbon seal 9
river dolphins 32
rockhopper penguin 7
Ross seal 6
royal albatross 7

royal angelfish 34

S
sailfin tang 13
sally lightfoot crab 13
saltwater crocodile 37
sanderlings 15
saola 33
sargassum crab 24
sargassum fish 24
sarus crane 33
sawfish 36
scallop 23
scuba diver 42
sea anemone 14, 15, 16, 21, 28
sea dandelion 16
sea gulls 14
seals
-Antarctic fur seal 41
-Cape fur seal 23
-crabeater seal 39, 40
-fur seal 10
-grey seal 23
-harp seal 9
-Hawaiian monk seal 13
-hooded seal 45
-leopard seal 40
-Mediterranean monk
  seal 23, 26
-Northern fur seal 13
-Pacific harbour seal 19
-ribbon seal 9
-Southern elephant
  seal 23, 39
sea lions 10, 14
sea nettle jellyfish 9
sea otter 13

sea slug 31
sea snail 15
sea star 14, 15, 35
sea turtles 25, 45
sea urchins 14, 18
seahorse 23, 26, 34
shark
-black-tipped reef
  shark 30
-blue shark 7
-frilled shark 13, 29
-goblin shark 28
-great white shark 13
-hammerhead shark 31
-lemon shark 23
-leopard shark 18
-porbeagle shark 24
-reef shark 20
-tiger shark 20
shearwaters 10
shore crab 15
short-tailed
  shearwaters 10
shrimp 16
skate 6
Southern
  elephant seal 23, 39
Southern right
  whale 23, 39
sperm whale 31
spider crab 27
spiny lobster 14, 26
spiny plunderfish 39
sponges 20, 21
spotted deer 36
spotted eagle ray 23, 30
spotted wolffish 7

Steller's sea eagle 44
striped dolphin 26
striped jellyfish 18
surgeon fish 21

T
Tawaki penguin 13
tiger shark 20
torpedo ray 18, 19
triggerfish 25
tuna
-bluefin tuna 23, 27
-yellowfin tuna 31
two-spot octopus 19

V
vampire squid 28
vaquita porpoise 45
vent crab 17
viperfish 29
volcano limpets 15

W
walrus 9, 44
wandering albatross 38
water monitor 33
Weddell seal 39
whales 26
-blue whale 6, 41
-bottlenose whale 39
-bowhead whale 9
-fin whale 26
-humpback whale 8, 11
-killer whale 13, 40
-minke whale 20
-Southern right whale
  23, 39

-sperm whale 31
whelks 15
white spotted
  jellyfish 13
white-sided dolphin 13
white-spotted
  octopus 27
willets 25
wolf eels 19
woolly sculpins 15

Y
yellow-bellied sea
  snake 31
yellowfin tuna 31
yeti crabs 16

Z
zoarcid fish 16
zooplankton 9